Growing Your Salon
on a
$100
Marketing Budget

From single chair to multi-station,
independent salons, chains and franchises.

Elizabeth Kraus
www.12monthsofmarketing.com

TABLE OF CONTENTS

5   foreword

7   introduction

10 making it count: channel overview

17 spending the money

    20 a closer look: word of mouth

    32 a closer look: SEO

    37 a closer look: online directories

    40 a closer look: email marketing

44 summary

45 bonus resources

46 post script, about the author

FOREWORD

Can you really grow your salon on just $100 per month?

In the pages that follow, I will answer that question by showing you how to grow your salon without a big marketing team or budget. Based on the most effective marketing channels, I'll show you what I would do to market a salon based on today's best practices.

I'll tell you in detail how I would spend a $100 marketing budget. I'll show you a detailed plan for social media (including a month's worth of sample social posts), email marketing, how to add content to your website that helps your salon get found online, and talk about the different ways networking and memberships can help you grow.

I'll get the job done quickly, and my plan will be on-budget and require less than half of the time-investment small business owners usually spend on marketing each month.

If you have questions for me when we're done, contact me using the form in the footer of my website at www.12monthsofmarketing.com.

Sincerely,

Elizabeth Kraus

86,000
Salons and Barber Shops
in the United States

1,100,000+
1.1 Million Licensed Pros

35,000
US cities and towns
2.5 to 1 Salon Competition
30 to 1 Stylist Competition

Growing Your Salon
on a $100 Marketing Budget:

INTRODUCTION

The U.S. Geological Survey recognizes 35,000 cities and towns; in which there are roughly 86,000 beauty establishments (82,000 salons and 4,000 barber shops) and more than 656,000 jobs (U.S. Bureau of Labor Statistics, 2014).

Other estimates for numbers of licensed beauty professionals in the United States are much higher; ProBeauty.org's 2012 Economic Snapshot puts the number of beauty professionals at nearly 1.1 million and more than 2 million when professionals with expired licenses are added.

If you're doing the math, that's roughly 2.5 pro beauty businesses (salons or barbershops) for every town or city in the United States. In areas of high urban density, a given salon would expect to find even more establishments directly competing against them for market share.

Considering the rise of the salon suite movement and the number of states where booth renting business models dominate, competition doesn't stop at salon vs. salon. Many stylists in the United States are independent business owners, competing not only with stylists across town at another salon but – in effect – against the other stylists in their own building as well.

Returning to the number of 35,000 U.S. cities and towns vs 1.1 million active beauty pros in the U.S., that puts competition at the individual stylist level at 30:1 – or higher if you include beauty pros with expired licenses.

Imagine for a moment that you're not competing for market share, but in a tug of war.

It's you on one end of the rope – and 30 or more other beauty pros on the other.

The size and weight of each competitor isn't based on diet and exercise, but on the amount of marketing and advertising each brings to the field.

How would you do? Probably many would answer: Not so hot.

When you look at the marketing and advertising your competitors have in the market, you even wonder how you can compete effectively – especially if you are an independent beauty pro leasing space or a suite.

Even if you're a salon owner, you're still outmatched in our game of marketing tug of war, based on the numbers of salons and salon suites you're competing against day in and day out.

Here's the good news:
Size doesn't matter.

As an independent beauty pro or salon owner, you can grow your business effectively on even a minimal budget.

It's not about the size of your bank account or your marketing department; it's about having a clear vision, the right tactics, and the will to execute a plan.

A Chamber of Commerce – BrightLocal October 2013 survey of more than 600 ChamberofCommerce.com members found that – on average – small and midsize businesses spend $400 a month on marketing.

However, responses varied; half of respondents spent less than $250 a month on marketing, one third of respondents spent $100 or less and a full 5 percent didn't spend anything at all.

That's a mere $100 total allocated to some **pretty important** marketing activities; things like:

(you are not alone)

33%

of small business owners spend $100 or less on marketing each month

- Brand Awareness
- Client Acquisition
- Customer Visit Frequency
- Average Sales Ticket
- Customer Retention
- Market share
- Mindshare

If you've only got $100 to spend on marketing each month, make it count.

Before we talk budget, let's talk about the marketing channels these same SMB (small and midsized business) owners say work best in helping them grow.

Making it Count: Most Effective Marketing Channels for Small-Medium Sized Businesses

You might still be skeptical whether all the marketing needed to grow your salon can truly be done on a $100 marketing budget, so let's see which marketing channels we need our plan to cover.

Based on the marketing channels small and medium-sized business owners said were most effective, the top four marketing channels (therefore the ones we need to focus on) are, in order of importance: word of mouth, SEO (search engine optimization), online directories and email marketing.

Let's take a closer look at each of these four most-effective marketing channels, starting with word of mouth, the marketing channel most widely-cited as their "best marketing" by business owners in every industry.

Source: BrightLocal and ChamberofCommerce.com survey
http://selnd.com/21tZFm1

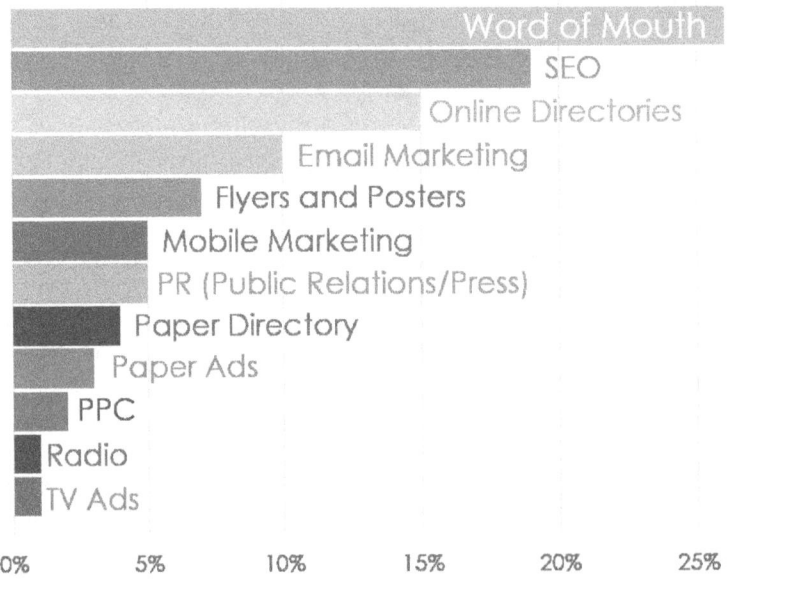

SMB Most Effective Client Acquisition Channels

1. Word of Mouth

By the Numbers: 75% of consumers say word of mouth is a key influencer in their purchasing decisions – and more than 25% of SMB say it's their most effective marketing. But what exactly is "word of mouth" marketing?

People who personally experience or who have some other reason to trust your brand recommend (referrals) or endorse it (reviews) to others.

Word of mouth often comes from customers, but not always. Anyone who knows about your salon and has any reason to feel it would be worthwhile for a friend, colleague, loved one, social follower, email subscriber, etc. might provide your salon with a word of mouth endorsement.

Online reviews are an especially powerful form of word of mouth marketing. In fact, 9 out of ten consumers trust online reviews just as much as they do personal referrals from people they know. Your salon could benefit from word of mouth in the form of:

- Personal referrals made to friends, colleagues, loved ones from customers, vendors, suppliers, or other people – anyone who knows about your salon
- Online reviews
- Social media check-ins, shares, selfies, shout outs and other implied and overt endorsements
- Networking events and organizations
- Marketing partners (cooperative marketing, talking about your salon or linking to your salon's website or social pages online)

2. SEO (Search Engine Optimization)

By the Numbers:

- 2011: 92% of U.S. adults who use the internet, use search engines (Pew Internet Study)
- 2015: More than 100 BILLION Google searches per month; more than half occurring on mobile devices
- 64% of all desktop search traffic and 89% of all mobile search traffic is on Google (www.internetlivestats.com)

What is SEO (Search Engine Optimization)?

Optimizing digital content and source code (web, blog, social, email, directory listings – any page a search engine like Google, Bing, Yahoo, etc. might "crawl") includes any and all tactics that make your website more likely to appear in an online search when someone is searching online for a business like yours, or for the type of content that is on your website.

We aren't going to explore how to optimize every aspect of a website or page in detail in this book; however, for those who want to get the most return on investment from time spent optimizing their website for search, I recommend the free MOZ. com Beginners Guide to SEO at https://moz.com/beginners-guide-to-seo.

3. Online Directories

By the Numbers: More than **90% of consumers** think more favorably of brands that **align with** their personal **values**. (dbsquaredinc.com/csr-policy514/).

What are Online Directories?

Anywhere your website is added to a searchable online directory which enhances your site's visibility and creates relevant inbound links to your website. For example:

- Earned and paid directory listings such as trade associations, sponsorships, affiliates, etc.
- Networking groups, Chambers of Commerce, Rotary and other civic organizations, community business listings, and so on

When a business demonstrates involvement in city, neighborhood and community organizations through memberships or by sponsoring causes which, in turn, list the business and its website in an online directory, they receive a valuable boost not only to SEO but public relations as well. These affiliations can also be invaluable resources for marketing partnerships, peer reviews and endorsements.

4. Email Marketing

By the Numbers: 7 out of ten US consumers prefer to receive information from and communicate with brands via email Spring Metrics (hospitalitynet.org/news/4072623.html)

What Constitutes "Email Marketing?"

- Newsletters
- "Drip" lead nurturing campaigns
- Special offers
- Events and invitations
- Pre and post-sale emails
- Company announcements (new employees, products, services)
- Corporate announcements and press releases

Essentially, email marketing occurs any time you use email to share information with or solicit information from clients or prospects. Year after year marketers say email marketing is their most effective channel for conversions; however, email marketing can be useful to any and all of the marketing priorities we identified earlier:

- Brand Awareness
- Client Acquisition
- Customer Visit Frequency
- Average Sales Ticket
- Customer Retention
- Market share
- Mindshare

One of the reasons email marketing so effective is that email is part of the U.S. adult consumer's way of life. U.S. adults spend 6.5 hours a week on email at home, work, and:

- While watching TV or at the movies (70%)
- In bed (52%)
- On vacation (50%)
- While on the phone (43%)
- While in the bathroom (42%) (ewwwww)
- While driving (18%)

Before we lay out how to spend our $100 on marketing, we have to talk about the other investment required for success in achieving your marketing goals: and that other investment is **time**.

According to The Mobile Marketer, 64% of small business owners also act as their own one-man marketing team, or as I like to refer to it, a "one man marketing band."

A 2014 Constant Contact study found that small business owners who "do the marketing" for their organization spend 20 hours each week – on average on marketing activities.

(you are not alone) small business owners spend an average of

20

hours on marketing each week

Twenty hours a week is roughly one half of a full time employee; if you're a salon owner or stylist who is wearing multiple hats, giving away half of your work day hours for marketing might be impossible.

If that's true for you and your salon, the good news is that the plan I'm going to lay out for the $100 marketing budget can be accomplished in 7-10 hours a week, half that of the average small business owners say they spend on marketing activities or even less.

Once your $100 marketing plan is up and running, you may find that you can use automation to trim the time down even more.

In more good news, marketing plans that integrate these most-effective marketing channels are highly successful. In the same BrightLocal / Chamber of Commerce study referenced earlier, business owners who execute a multi-channel marketing plan see results like these:

- 73% achieved more engagement (retention/frequency/avg. ticket)
- 57% acquired new customers (acquisition/market share/brand awareness)
- 54% attracted more web traffic (brand awareness/customer acquisition)
- 42% increased event attendance (acquisition/retention/brand awareness)
- 40% made more revenue (MONEY!!! Market share/avg. ticket/frequency)
- 39% increased referrals (word of mouth/acquisition/brand awareness)

Which Brings Us to the Bottom Line:
Let's $pend the Money

Can we really accomplish word of mouth marketing, SEO, get listed in online directories and email clients and prospects – all on a $100 per month marketing budget?

Yes, yes we can; here's how*:

$9 -$29   Word of mouth (free; well, sort of)

$10   Organic SEO (free + cost of website hosting)

$33   Online directories (you'll see)

$20   Email marketing (cost of platform)

That totals up to $72 - 92 per month.

Not only can we do it all for $100, we've got money left over;
let's spend it!

Costs quoted in content as of March 2016, author bears no responsibility for pricing changes made by vendors referenced herein subsequent to publication, nor for user experience on vendor platforms. In all cases, vendors suggested are vendors the author is currently using personally in marketing activities.

So that you can see how each of these tasks might play out during the month, let's create a fictitious hair salon located near my hometown of Bonney Lake, Washington called "HAIR." We're going to talk about how HAIR salon spent their marketing money and time over the course of one month: April 2016.

The Hair And Image Revival (a.k.a. HAIR) is a Bonney Lake, WA all-ages salon whose stylists are especially great with fashion-forward women's hair styles and color services.

At the beginning of April 2016, their $100 marketing budget is allocated this way:

- $10 WordPress web hosting on 1and1.com at $9.99 per month (http://bit.ly/22AvMX4)
- $9 social media automation at www.hootsuite.com
- $20 email marketing using the campaigner.com platform (http://bit.ly/1So2PFU)
- $33 Online directories and networking (cost of Chamber membership plus monthly luncheon event)

+ Spending the Money Left Over

- $8 Giveaway (salon cost of retail product or gift card)
- $20 Facebook hyper-local sponsored post

Not only does HAIR have to spend their $100 marketing budget carefully, they also have to decide how they will spend the time they have allocated to marketing activities. Using Clients Rule: 2016 Marketing Calendar for Beauty Pros as a guide, they laid out their marketing plan for the month as you'll see on the following pages.

Their marketing plan for April encompasses all four of the top marketing channels small business owners say work best in growing a business: word of mouth, SEO, online directories and email marketing. The following summarizes their activities; however, each will be described in more detail in "Let's Take a Closer Look" sections that follow.

$9-29 per month Word of Mouth: HAIR salon posts updates on social media and monitors networks for engagement 6 days each week, Monday through Saturday. They also have strategies in place that help them:

- accumulate online reviews
- add new social followers
- get likes and shares on social networks
- add new email subscribers (current and prospective clients)

$10 per month SEO: HAIR adds new search-optimized content to its website every week (specific examples are included on the following pages). They understand how to optimize social posts for search, knowing how social link clicks and email link clicks help them drive web traffic that boosts their SEO efforts even more.

$33 per month Online Directories: HAIR participates in their local Chamber of Commerce. The online directory link back to their website boosts their SEO efforts and is another way that local residents discover their salon. In addition, they leverage their membership to drive brand awareness and marketing partners.

$20 per month Email Marketing: HAIR sends two emails to their full contact list during the month in addition to personalized email marketing messages based on client activity which will be described in more detail in the email marketing section to follow.

Let's Take a Closer Look: Word of Mouth

Cost: $37 per month + 1-2 Hours per week

- $9 Hootsuite.com pro membership
- $20 Facebook sponsored post
- $8 Giveaway item

Why Hootsuite?

Hootsuite helps HAIR's owner save a lot of time posting on social media. They use the platform to schedule their social media posts days in advance. By creating a list of things they want to post ahead of time and scheduling them to go out during the week, they ensure a steady stream of social media updates that will interest and engage their audience members.

Using Hootsuite also helps HAIR save time monitoring social media because they can see all of their social feeds in one dashboard. They can also react right from the platform with likes, replies and re-shares when their content is shared, liked or their salon is mentioned in social media.

They started using Hootsuite for free, but it only allowed them to link 3 profiles. By upgrading to the $9 per month Pro platform, they were able to add all of the salon's social profiles in plus the social media profiles the salon owner and stylists use for professional as well as personal posts.

Scheduling social posts days or weeks ahead of time with an automation tool like Hootesuite makes your social media profiles look more professional, active, consistent – even fun. It also enables you to post updates at the times of day when you are most likely to reach your target audiences – even if you're working or unable to be on social media at that time.

While you're working behind the chair or running your salon, social media can be working on your behalf to drive traffic to your website, appointment bookings, engagement and brand awareness.

Why Sponsor Posts on Facebook?

When HAIR sponsors a post on Facebook, they extend its reach to thousands more people that fit within their target market each month.

This helps build brand awareness; and, since Facebook's ad platform allows HAIR to target its advertising by city, zip code, gender, age and other interests, it has been very effective at only putting their posts in front of the people who represent their ideal client types.

Why a Giveaway Item?

HAIR gives away a retail product or styling tool each month. This gives them an opportunity to entice people to like and share a social post, follow their page or subscribe to email newsletters for a chance to win.

Let's take an even closer look at how social media, Hootsuite. com, Facebook sponsored post and a giveaway item work to build brand awareness, drive appointment bookings and add social followers and email subscribers, by seeing what they posted on social media in the month of April 2016.

Fri Apr 1	AM	Who Wore Their Hair Best at Last Month's Oscars? Via @ Elle #fashion #bonneylake at http://bit.ly/1nOzmtz
	PM	Going to TOLO? Looking for a Bonney Lake Salon that Does Updo's? Call 253-555-HAIR or book online at http://ourfakelink.com #auburnriverside #bonneylake #sumner-townusa
Sat Apr 2	AM	What Women Can Do About Hair Loss http://huff.to/1pLJ01J P.S., We can help, call 253-555-HAIR and book your free consultation with our #FHPL experts in #bonney-lake

Mon Apr 4	AM	Top 10 Foods for Healthy Hair via @WebMD http://wb.md/1UzD5rY #bonneylake #auburn #sumner
	PM	Who Knows How Bonney Lake WA Got Its Name? Leave your answer below, everyone who comments will be entered in our month-end $50 salon gift card drawing! #bonneylake
Tue Apr 5	AM	11 Celebrities Who've Gone Gray on Purpose via @instyle #haircolor #bonneylake at http://bit.ly/1RmK2Hw
	PM	Did you know? <brand name> mousse styling product is our product of the month! Everyone who likes and shares this post will be automatically entered for a chance to win a full-size mousse! Can't wait? Mention this promo in the salon and get your own at 25% off.
Wed Apr 6	AM	Best Looks from the 2016 Kids' Choice Awards Orange Carpet via @Instyle http://bit.ly/1o9MBoV #celebritystyles #bonneylake
	PM	Going to TOLO? Looking for a Bonney Lake Salon that Does Updo's? Call 253-555-HAIR or book online at http://ourfakelink.com #auburnriverside #bonneylake #sumnertownusa
Thu Apr 7	AM	What's Your Worst Pet Peeve? Today is "I'm Not Going to Take it Anymore Day," share your rant below! Everyone who plays along will be entered in our month-end $50 gift card drawing to use at one of the best salons in Bonney Lake!
	PM	Cosmetologist Confessions: 10 Reasons You Shouldn't Use Box Color http://bit.ly/21JAegB
Fri Apr 8	AM	This never happens! Last minute color opening on the books tomorrow at 10:30 AM – Who wants it? Call 253-555-HAIR ASAP for the best hair color services in Bonney Lake WA #HAIRsalon
Sat Apr 2	AM	Mention this promo in the salon and get your own at 25% off our <brand name> mousse styling product – it's our product of the month here at HAIR, the best salon in Bonney Lake!

Mon Apr 11	AM	Today is Pet Day! Share a picture of your favorite furry friend below, everyone who does gets entered into our month-end $50 Bonney Lake salon gift card drawing!
	PM	Oooh! Have you seen this Pinterest board of Easy Mom Hairstyles? Love! Which one is your favorite? http://bit.ly/22J6wL4 - P.S. Let us know if you'd like one of these looks in #bonneylake!!
Tue Apr 12	AM	Did you know? Cucumbers, fish and celery are the most hydrating foods for dry skin and hair in #bonneylake! http://huff.to/22J76s1
	PM	We got <client name> to try our <best hydrating conditioning product or service> today, here's what she said: <insert testimonial about product or service>
Wed Apr 13	AM	Find out what our Bonney Lake salon team members said brought them to work or live in Bonney Lake WA on our blog at http://ourfakelink.com
	PM	Mother's Day is just a month away! Get mom a HAIR salon gift card and plan to take her to one of our staff picks for Best Mother's Day Brunch in Bonney Lake, Buckley and Sumner – you'll find the list on our blog at http://ourfakelink.com
Thu Apr 14	AM	Today is Moment of Laughter Day – Share your best (or worst) joke below and then share this post with your networks! Everyone who plays along will be entered in our month-end $50 salon gift card drawing!
	PM	Best Bonney Lake Salon Moment of Laughter Day - Our stylist <name> said the funniest thing that a client ever said to her was <insert staff story here>
Fri Apr 15	AM	Meet <NAME> our newest stylist! New clients booking with her get 25% off all client services at HAIR salon in Bonney Lake during her first 30 days. Book now by calling <phone no> or using our online booking tool <link>
Sat Apr 16	AM	Even the best blow-out and style can be a hot mess after you've slept on it, here are 6 ways to protect your hair at night. http://bit.ly/1XSLvdq

Mon Apr 18	AM	Mention this promo in the salon and get your own at 25% off our <brand name> mousse styling product – it's our product of the month!
	PM	Ready Set Style! Which of these 2016 Summer Hair Trends do you want us to help you get for summer in Bonney Lake? http://on.today.com/1UNWqH8 Comment and share this post to enter our month-end $50 salon gift card drawing!
Tue Apr 19	AM	Yum! 10 Superfoods for Spring to Power Up Your Diet Right Here in Bonney Lake http://bit.ly/1UpKLPg #bonney-lake #sumnertownusa
	PM	This coming Saturday is our Spring Look Saturday! Stop by our Bonney Lake salon Saturday morning between the hours of AM and 1 PM for expert advice from <esthetician's name> who will be giving 5 minute touchups in spring eyeshadow and lip colors – everyone who participates will be entered to win a spring eyeshadow of their choice!
Wed Apr 20	AM	HAIR is one of the best salons in Bonney Lake WA because we make – and keep – promises to our clients! You'll find our client promises on our website at http://ourfake-link.com
	PM	Today is Banana Day! DID YOU KNOW that the Vitamin C and B6 found in bananas help maintain the integrity and elasticity of the skin? Now you do! #bonneylake #haircare
Thu Apr 21	AM	Spring Look Saturday is just 2 DAYS AWAY! Come in to our Bonney Lake salon Saturday between the hours of AM and 1 PM for a free 5-minute makeup touchup in spring eyeshadow and lip colors – everyone who participates will be entered to win a spring eyeshadow of their choice!
	PM	Like and share this post for a chance to win an 8 oz <brand name> mousse styling product – it's HAIR salon's best product of the month!
Fri Apr 22	AM	TOMORROW IS our Spring Look Saturday! Stop by our Bonney Lake salon Saturday morning between the hours of AM and 1 PM for expert advice from <esthetician's name> and 5 minute touchups in spring eyeshadow and lip colors + a chance to win a spring eyeshadow of your choice!
Sat Apr 23	AM	TODAY IS Spring Look Saturday! Stop by our Bonney Lake salon Saturday morning between the hours of AM and 1 PM for expert advice from <esthetician's name> and 5 minute touchups in spring eyeshadow and lip colors + achance to win a spring eyeshadow of your choice!

Mon Apr 25	AM	What's coming next month? So glad you asked!! Find out what our contests, giveaway, promo and products of the month are for May, and don't forget to pick up a HAIR salon gift card for mom for Mother's Day!
	PM	Ooh la la! 26 Celeb photos show off 2016 hair color trends to inspire your next hair color appointment at http://bit.ly/1WOkZlj -- Which is your favorite, and which one do you wish you had the guts to ask for? Everyone who comments below and shares this post with their friends will be automatically entered in our month-end $50 salon gift card drawing!
Tue Apr 26	AM	Mention this promo in the salon and get your own at 25% off our <brand name> mousse styling product – it's our product of the month!
	PM	HAIR's Bonney Lake salon staff weighed in with 10 hair and makeup shortcuts perfect for every office worker! Read the whole list on our blog at http://ourfakelink.com
Wed Apr 27	AM	In honor of Admin Pros Day we found this Pinterest board filled with office-ready hairstyles. Which will you ask for at your next appointment? http://bit.ly/1MGVigM As usual, everyone who comments below and shares this post with their friends will be automatically entered in our month-end $50 salon gift card drawing!
	PM	HAIR salon gift cards are the perfect Mother's Day gift in #bonneylake, now even better – get 2x the referral rewards when you buy a gift card for mom to use in our Bonney Lake salon for Mother's Day!
Thu Apr 28	AM	Today is cubicle day! Share photos of how you've decorated your workspace below. Everyone who comments below and shares this post with their friends will be automatically entered in our month-end $50 salon gift card drawing!
	PM	Congratulations to <Saturday's spring makeup eyeshadow winner> who won a <brand name> <color name> eyeshadow; be sure that you check out our spring eyeshadow and lip colors in the salon in Bonney Lake – while they last!
Fri Apr 29	AM	Get weekend makeup inspiration! See summer 2016 hair and makeup trends http://bit.ly/22A86IN to wear around the world or right here in #BonneyLake
Sat Apr 30	AM	Like and share this post for a chance to win an 8 oz <brand name> mousse styling product – it's our product of the month and the drawing happens MONDAY!

Here are some things I want to bring to your attention relative to the social media plan above.

1. Very few of the posts are promoting the salon in an advertising style. Most stimulate engagement and provide incentives (chance to win, etc.) for people to participate.

2. The list above was written in 3 hours of working time. That's a whole month's worth of social media accomplished in just a few hours of time. It is possible to have a strong social media marketing program without investing a lot of time, or constantly going in and out of the program when you automate posting with a program like Hootsuite.

You can choose the time, date and which of the salon or personal social profiles connected to the account where any social update should be published.

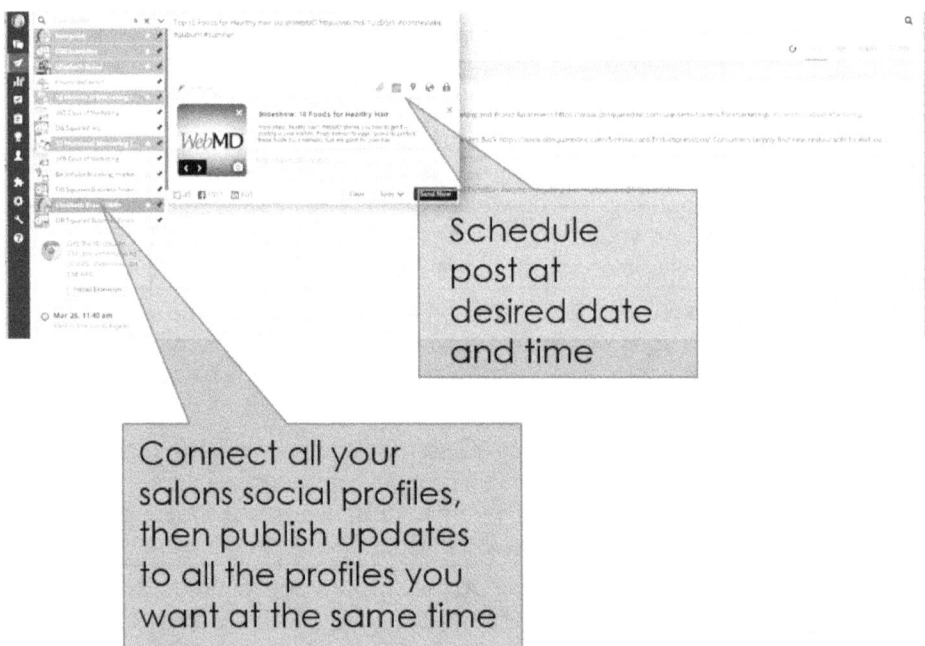

Schedule post at desired date and time

Connect all your salons social profiles, then publish updates to all the profiles you want at the same time

You can monitor all of the salon's social platforms in one place to see what is in the feed in real time and monitor social platforms for mentions as a brand reputation and engagement tool.

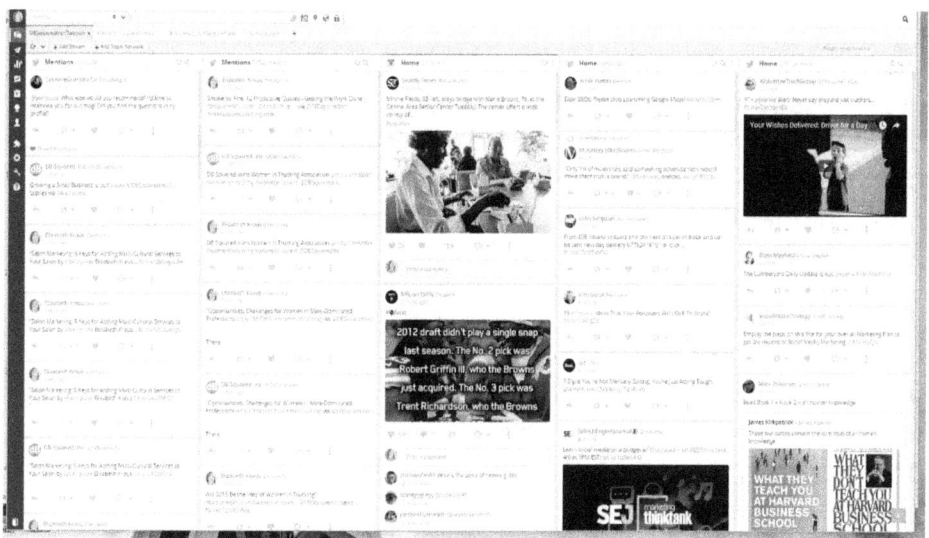

3. In addition to Hootsuite, HAIR salon uses Bitly.com to create what are sometimes called short links. Bitly.com is a FREE program you can use to shorten website links. This is important for many reasons: (a) They take up less room and (b) don't detract from the real message you want people to see.

Plus, when you use a URLshortener like Bitly (c) you havethe ability to see how many times any of these links were clicked. This tells you what type of content is most popular with your audiences, so you can infuse more of the content that engages your target markets into your social strategy.

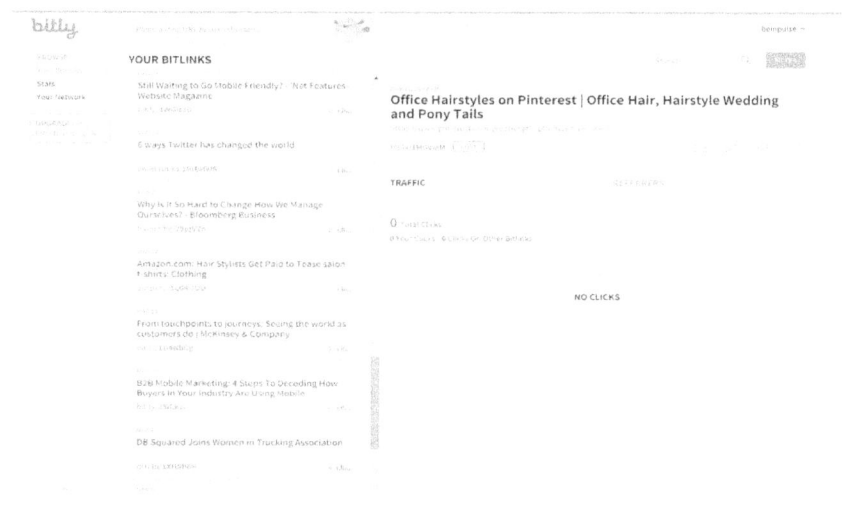

4. Many of HAIR's social posts have key phrases that help even their social posts appear in search results. These key phrases are words real people might type into a search engine to find a salon in Bonney Lake or who are looking for other types of online content (such as Mother's Day gift ideas or a retail product line's brand name) that could help local people who don't already know about HAIR discover them — building brand awareness and more word of mouth.

5. #hashtags are another tool that help HAIR's updates show up more often in search results and (in particular) on social networks like Twitter and Instagram where users look for businesses and online content by hashtag.

HAIR salon even has their own hashtag - #HAIRsalon - for followers to use in shares, retweets and for the purposes of other social media contests, events and drawings.

6. Since HAIR salon adds a new blog post to their website every Tuesday, Wednesday's social posts promote blog content and help drive traffic back to the salon's website.

When this happens, search engines like Google perceive the salon's website to have more authority and relevance, which helps them to move up in search rankings when people are looking for salons in Bonney Lake via online search.

$20 Sponsored Post on Facebook

While $20 does not go a long way in pay-per-click advertising on other platforms, it can provide a significant boost on Facebook.

Facebook ad's platform allows users to target ads in such a way that only the people they really want to see the ad will see it and have a chance to click on it– ad dollars spent here can be very effective.

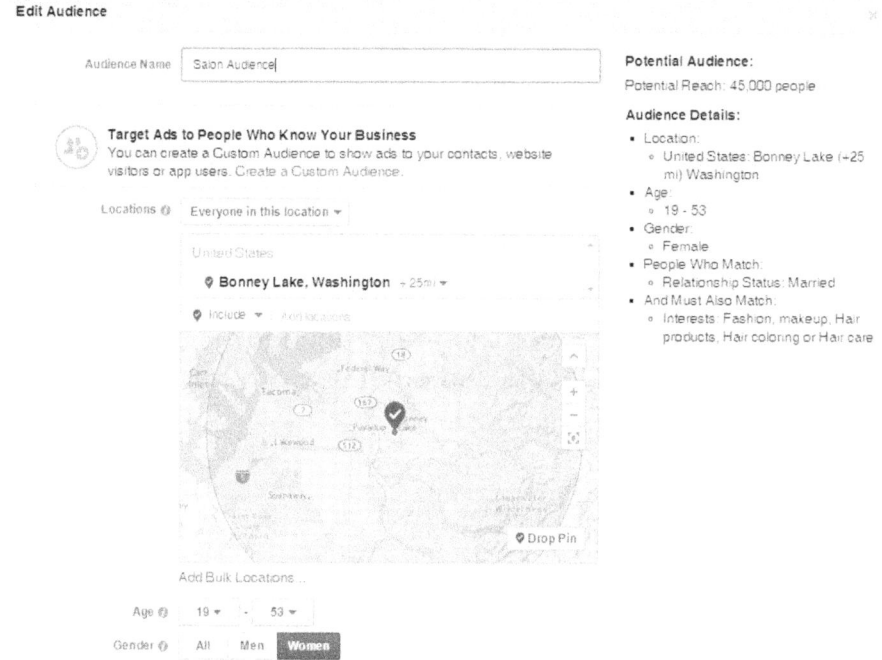

In April, HAIR salon decided to use the $20 they have allocated to spend on Facebook sponsored posts this month to promote a specific post from April 1.

HAIR decides that since many salons in Bonney Lake refuse to do Updo's for school dances that they'll will spend $20 to sponsor this post on Facebook.

Going to TOLO? Looking for a Bonney Lake Salon that Does Updo's? **Call 253-555-HAIR or book online at** http://ourfakelink.com
#auburnriverside #bonneylake #sumnertownusa

Doing so extends the post reach to thousands more local residents (brand awareness and mindshare) since Facebook ads can be targeted to people city by city, by gender, and age group. Hyper-local targeted means that only members of the ad's target audience will see it and the clicks will be likely to convert (client acquisition).

The additional web traffic coming from Facebook is also a positive SEO signal to Google and other search engines.

And that's not all.

Social Check In, Tagging and Before-After Salon Client Photos

HAIR's owner realizes that staff can – and must be – instrumental in helping extend the salon's reach on Facebook and Instagram.

When stylists welcome a guest they invite them to check in on Facebook. There are also signs in the waiting area and near the hair dryers asking clients to check in and suggesting which hashtags to use for the salon and stylist.

Stylists are held accountable to post at least one "after" client photo, tagging client and salon, for every 4 appointments. When they do, they earn points that can be used toward continuing education classes, VISA gift cards, or scholarships offset the cost of attending national beauty shows and conferences.

Clients who participate are automatically entered into a month-end $50 salon gift card drawing to use at their next appointment. At the end of each month, clients who win are recognized in email, blog news and on social media as the "client of the month" (and tagged yet again).

Every time clients are tagged on social networks, posts can potentially reach all of their friends and loved ones, too.

And even that's not all.

Online Salon Reviews

Knowing that today's shoppers trust online reviews just as much as personal recommendations, HAIR's owner makes online reviews a cornerstone of the customer experience.

At the point of sale, every customer is invited to use the salon's tablet and Wi-Fi to go online and leave a review for the salon or their stylist; once every 4 appointments they also receive an email inviting them to do the same thing.

Let's Take a Closer Look:
SEO (Search Engine Optimization)

Cost: $10 per month + 3 hours per week

Web hosting with 1and1.com is $9.99 per month (for the first year) which includes:

- 1 domain name
- unlimited number of email addresses – everyone on staff can have an email address that ends in the salon's domain name; such as elizabeth@HAIRbonneylake.com
- complies with Googles preference for SSL certificate
- is managed for updates
- allows for multiple WordPress projects and unlimited storage (SSD)

The monthly hosting cost of 1and1.com is the only cost – apart from time – that HAIR salon invests in SEO. While there are booking platforms that let salons build web pages and free platforms that let businesses build out whole websites, HAIR salon understands that they need their own website, with their own unique URL.

Why?

If HAIR salon built their web pages on a booking platform or a "free" website hosting platform, they can't get the most marketing impact out of their online efforts. Web content HAIR publishes on those sites drives web traffic and lends authority and relevance to the hosting platform (as far as search engines are concerned), not HAIR's brand.

They are competing for the same web traffic with any other salon using that platform, especially other salons in their city or region.

They are diluting their brand identity and message.

Most of these platforms don't give users the ability to change the META title, description and keywords housed in web page source code which tell search engines what a web page is about – and which are an indispensable part of search optimization.

Here's what I recommend to my clients - and use myself.

A hosted site set up on WordPress ($299 per year + Cost of adding SSL Certificate) or a WordPress website hosted on 1and1.com (http://bit.ly/22AvMX4) at $9.99 per month (for the first year).

The 1and1.com WordPress hosted site package includes one domain name (e.g., HAIRsalon.com) and meets Google's preference for a website with security certificate – Google has said they give preference in search results to websites which are:

- Mobile-friendly, responsive web site – responsive sites automatically detect the user's device type and displays in a way that is optimized for the device (smartphone, PC, tablet, etc.)

- Has an adequate SSL Certificate (SSL Certificates are small data files that allow for secure connections from a web server to a browser).

- Filled with quality content real people want to read, view, etc.

- Optimized for search with relevant key words and phrases "real people" might type into a Google search to find that type of organization – without being keyword-stuffed.

For more guidance on optimizing a web site to make it more likely to get found in online search, MOZ.com's Beginner's Guide to SEO at https://moz.com/beginners-guide-to-seo is an outstanding, easy to understand tutorial.

Why WordPress?

A responsive WordPress website will meet Google's standards for best practices from the get-go. Plus, there are so many ready-to-use templates from free to less than $100 -- even amateur website managers will be able to get a site set up fairly quickly. Best of all, the WordPress platform is so popular that thousands of developers build what are called "plugins" for the site, including:

- form creators that make it easy to insert registration and subscription forms on web pages
- SEO tools like the YOAST SEO plugin that make it easy to optimize page tags without any programming
- spam-filters that automatically blog form spam
- PayPal plugins that let you sell online without a web store

—and many more. Check out this list of 24 "must have" plugins for new businesses at http://bit.ly/1PvwcBq.

Let's take an even closer look at how HAIR salon updates their website to get found online, more often, in online search in the month of April 2016.

HAIR salon uses the web site and blog ideas provided in Clients Rule: 2016 Marketing Calendar for Salon and Spa to power their SEO efforts and provide content they can share on social media and email marketing newsletters. You'll see how it all works together in the website content publishing schedule that follows.

Cost: $10 per month for hosting plus 3 hours of content creation and publishing time each week

Published Tuesday, April 5 — 600-800 word blog post titled:
Bonney Lake Salons: What's New at HAIR Salon in April 2016
listing HAIR's April 2016 promotion details (services and products) with the key phrase Bonney Lake salons used 2-3 times in the article and once each in the blog post's meta title and description (super-easy to do in WordPress via the Yoast plugin!).

Published Tuesday, April 12 — 600-800 word blog post titled:
What Clients Can Expect at the Best Salons in Bonney Lake
talking about what first-time clients can expect when they visit your salon and a list of client promises with the key phrase best salons in Bonney Lake used 2-3x in the article and once each in the blog post's meta title and description.

Published Tuesday, April 19 — 600-800 word blog post titled:
HAIR Salon in Bonney Lake Best Office Hair Styles
with hair, make up and style tips for office workers in honor of Administrative Professional's Day (April 27) which includes the key phrase HAIR salon in Bonney Lake 2-3x in the article and once each in the blog post's meta title and description.

Published Tuesday, April 26 — 600-800 word blog post titled:
Top 10 Best Mothers Day Brunch in Bonney Lake
including spots in Bonney Lake, Sumner, Buckley (cities where the salon's target markets reside) with the key phrase Best Mothers Day Brunch in Bonney Lake used 2-3 times in the article and once each in the blog post's meta title and description.

Completing these four assignments means the salon adds four new web pages with content their readers will love to their website every month – content that has keywords that can help people looking for a salon in the Bonney Lake area to find HAIR in search results.

In addition, adding local-interest articles – like a list of best places to go on Mothers Day for brunch – can help the salon get discovered by a wider local audience, building brand awareness among local residents and turning the salon website into a valuable resource not only for people who visit the site, but for businesses that the salon includes in these feature articles. These types of marketing partnerships can be very powerful in generating cross-marketing referrals and additional web traffic.

Here's something else to consider.

All the work HAIR salon does to get found online is that much more effective because few of their competitors have websites at all! The ones who do have websites don't add content very often and their content doesn't include many keywords.

In fact, Most of HAIR's competitors try to use their Facebook page instead of a website, not realizing that they are missing out on the single most important component of any small business marketing strategy: the web site.

By adding content once a week, HAIR salon quickly climbs to the top of search results – so it's the first salon in the list when anyone searches for a hair salon in Bonney Lake and surrounding cities.

HAIR salon also adds one more blog post at the end of each month that congratulates winners of its social media drawings for product giveaway and salon card giveaway. This is another type of web content that puts the spotlight on products or services. Plus, winners can be tagged in updates on social media, extending the salon's brand reach out to their client's followers as well.

Let's Take a Closer Look:
Online Directories

Cost: $33 per month + 2-3 hours per week
— monthly cost of HAIR salon's membership in The Chamber Collective, the community's Chamber of Commerce, plus the member-cost of attending the Chamber's monthly luncheon.

Chamber of Commerce membership provides HAIR salon with a valuable backlink from the Chamber of Commerce website –another boost to their website's SEO with Google and other search engines since a city's Chamber of Commerce website will be one that search algorithms consider "high quality."

Membership in the Chamber also means that HAIR salon is listed in all of the print directories and programs published by the Chamber each year for distribution to the public or use at Chamber events.

Not only does Chamber membership help with brand awareness, it tells people in the community that HAIR salon is involved in community-building events and organizations for additional word of mouth and social proof.

As a Chamber member, HAIR salon also has the opportunity to network with other business owners and propose marketing partnerships for shared website links – more valuable backlinks that help boost SEO and build brand awareness. Here are some of the networking opportunities they take advantage of each month:

- Tuesday morning networking group of 25-35 business owners 1x monthly
- 1x monthly luncheon with guest speaker and networking opportunities
- 1x monthly Good Morning Bonney Lake educational networking event
- 1x monthly after hours networking event hosted by a Chamber member
- Ribbon Cutting and Grand Openings for new businesses
- Annual walk-a-thon, summer city fair and Music on the Lake events

HAIR also partners with other Chamber members who have the same target markets. HAIR salon features their marketing partners with a backlink or even a whole blog post on its website, email newsletters or in social media updates, and vice versa.

Some of HAIR's marketing partners even let the salon place copies of their business cards and menus in their waiting and point of sale areas, giving the salon a chance to introduce itself to their customers.

Chamber of Commerce memberships (and memberships in similar organizations), sponsorships and other activities that provide HAIR salon with an online directory listing aren't just about networking or giving back:

They help to fulfil the top SMB marketing tactic for listings in online directories. These backlinks send a valuable SEO signal to search engines that the salon's website is more important than competitor sites they might serve up in online search results.

Community and group activity helps build brand awareness and become another potential word of mouth referral source.

These groups also give you the opportunity to create marketing partnerships or do joint marketing activities with other businesses that share your target markets.

Membership gives HAIR Salon insider information and a voice in city politics, regulations and business-related events. Chamber membership is often a great stepping stone to Chamber and city leadership positions as well.

Let's Take a Closer Look:
Email Marketing

Cost: $20 per month + 1-2 hours per week

$19.99 per month using Campaigner.com
(unlimited emails up to 1,000 contacts)

Not only is Email marketing listed as a top marketing channel in the BrightLocal/ChamberofCommerce study referenced earlier in this resource, it also comes in at the top of the list of most effective client acquisition marketing channel year after year for both retail and B2B organizations, in multiple surveys.

Let's take an even closer look at how HAIR salon used email marketing to drive bookings, client education, web traffic and client engagement in the month of April.

HAIR salon uses the email marketing ideas provided in Clients Rule: 2016 Marketing Calendar for Salon and Spa to power their email marketing efforts.

They have two emails that go out to all contacts every month, but that's not the only way they use email to build business. Here's a list of the emails they sent in April.

1st Day of the Month (30 minutes) – All Contacts

Special email announcing social media salon gift card and mousse product give away winners.

1st Wednesday of the Month (2 Hours) – All Contacts

Email with link to new web/blog content, April salon promotions and Mother's Day gift card, events and highlighting details of one new products or services, reminder to follow on social networks (with links) for special social media only contests and announcements.

2nd Wednesday Every Other Month (1 Hour) – Segment of Contacts

A special "we miss you" email is sent to clients who have not come back in the past 60 days.

3rd Wednesday of the Month (2 Hours) – All Contacts

Email with link to new web / blog content, last chance reminder about expiring promotions and Mother's Day gift cards, and a preview of May's promotions.

4th Wednesday of the Month (2 hours) – All Contacts

Special email promoting Mother's Day gift cards as part of a list of – and with subject line of – Top 10 Mother's Day Ideas in Bonney Lake; this list is added as an extra blog post for HAIR salon's website as well. The list references 2-3 restaurants serving Mother's Day brunch, salon gift card and suggested services, local trails for hiking with outdoorsy moms, local parks with family-friendly facilities, boutiques with specialty retail, etc.

And that's not all.

Every client on the books provides an email address for pre and post-appointment emails, and a mobile number for SMS day-before appointment reminders; compliance earns them another entry in the salon's month end gift card drawing.

In addition to client engagement, email reminders are vital to the salons profitability in cutting down no-shows and stimulating re-booking more frequently.

Stylists are held accountable to either obtain or confirm the client's email address at every appointment, and earn points for doing so.

The salon also uses geo-targeted, promoted social media updates for gift card and product giveaways that require contact information to further build their email contact database outside of their client base.

And even that's not all.

3-4 days after a client's appointment, they receive an email from the salon that rotates between four different themes:

- Asking if the client has any concerns or questions for the salon about their experience or if happy encouraged to go online (link provided) and leave a review
- Personal thank you text written by their stylist
- Link to a customer satisfaction survey; all participants are automatically entered into the month end $25 gift card drawing
- Reminder about the salon's referral reward program and how to participate

E.g., 3-4 days after April's appointment, client would receive an email asking about their questions or concerns (the first bullet point). 3-4 days after their May/June appointment, this client receives an email with a personal note from their stylist (the second bullet point), and so on, so that the most a client ever sees any one type of email is 1-2x per year, depending on how often they rebook.

And even that's not all.

Two weeks after for men and three weeks after appointments for women, a client receives an email with a reminder (plus link to booking platform) to book their next appointment; or, if pre-booked, a reminder about their next appointment and invitation to reply with any concerns or special requests, especially if the client needs to book extended time for a new style.

Email marketing is a powerful way to build brand awareness, cut down on no-shows, generate client referrals and keep HAIR salon top of mind with clients when it comes time to rebook, buy gift cards, get in on salon contests and events, and so on. Plus:

- Email is the preferred brand communication channel of consumers
- Web traffic driven from the salon's email to their web site (blog articles, product pages, etc.,) also helps to boost SEO by telling search engines that the website is active, relevant and interesting to real people
- Emails with value-added content (fashion, hair, style, holiday lists, etc.,) become more sharable on social networks and forwards to other friends or colleagues who might be interested – making them a word of mouth tactic

SUMMARY: The Real Cost of a $100 Marketing Budget

$100 in money
+ 30-35 hours in time per month

Less than half of the 20 hours per week small business owners devote to marketing activities on average, while hitting all of the most effective marketing channels in the process –

- Word of mouth
- SEO
- Online directories
- Email marketing

BONUS RESOURCES FOR SALON MARKETING

Clients Rule: 2016 Marketing Calendar for Salon and Spa
http://12monthsofmarketing.com/2016-marketing-calendars-salon/

The ABC's of Salon Client Retention
http://12monthsofmarketing.com/salon-client-retention-abcs/
+ hundreds of other salon marketing articles on my blog at
12monthsofmarketnig.com.

Salon and spa marketing, leadership and other resources
at https://www.dbsquaredinc.com/category/salon-and-spa/
such as:

- Ideas for a Salon Cell Phone Policy that Won't Turn Clients Off
- 6 Salon Holiday Marketing Ideas Get the Attention of Holiday Shoppers
- 3 Places You Shouldn't Skimp for a Salon or Salon Franchise – and more

POST SCRIPT

I hope that the content of this e-book helped you – whether you needed a whole plan or just needed to tweak your existing marketing to make it better.

If you have questions for me, are interested in hearing this presentation as a workshop or keynote, or you would like information about the services available from my company, contact me using the form in the footer of my website at www.12monthsofmarketing.com.

Sincerely,

Elizabeth Kraus

About the Author

Elizabeth Kraus is a freelance marketing consultant with more than ten years experience working with members of the professional beauty industry including distributors, product manufacturers, salon and spa owners and stylists. You might also like:

- Clients Rule: 2016 Marketing Calendar for Salons
- Make Over Your Marketing: 12 Months of Marketing for Salon and Spa
- 365 Days of Marketing

Residing in the greater Seattle area, Kraus offers local and virtual marketing services to organizations in B2B as well as direct-to-consumer industries.

www.ingramcontent.com/pod-product-compliance
Lightning Source LLC
Chambersburg PA
CBHW080642190526
45169CB00009B/3466